Collective Biographies

UNION GENERALS

OF THE

CIVIL WAR

Carl R. Green and
William R. Sandford

E **Enslow Publishers, Inc.**
44 Fadem Road   PO Box 38
Box 699   Aldershot
Springfield, NJ 07081 Hants GU12 6BP
USA   UK

Library of Congress Cataloging-in-Publication Data

Green, Carl R.
    Union generals of the Civil War / Carl R. Green & William R. Sanford.
        p. cm.—(Collective biographies)
    Includes bibliographical references and index.
    Summary: Profiles ten Union generals: Ambrose Burnside, Ulysses S. Grant, Henry Halleck, Winfield Scott Hancock, Joseph Hooker, George McClellan, George Meade, Philip Sheridan, William T. Sherman, and George Henry Thomas.
    ISBN 0–7660–1028–7
    1. Generals—United States—Biography—Juvenile literature.
    2. United States. Army—Biography—Juvenile literature. 3. United States—History—Civil War, 1861–1865—Biography—Juvenile literature. [1. Generals. 2. United States—History—Civil War, 1861–1865—Biography.] I. Sanford, William R. II. Title. III. Series.
    E467.S275   1998
    973.7'41'0922—dc21
    [B]   97-27998
                                                                          CIP
                                                                          AC

Printed in the United States of America

10 9 8 7 6 5 4 3 2 1

Illustration Credits: Digital Stock Historical pp. 12, 18, 22, 28, 37, 43, 53, 58, 64, 76, 81, 84, 91, 100; Enslow Publishers, Inc., p. 8; National Archives pp. 30, 40, 48, 66, 94; Carl R. Green and William R. Sanford, p. 73.

Cover Illustration: Library of Congress

Contents

Introduction

On April 12, 1861, Southern guns opened fire on Fort Sumter, South Carolina. The deadly barrage set off the Civil War. Generals of the North and South led troops through four years of fierce, bloody battles. By the time the guns fell silent, 620,000 Americans had died in a struggle to determine the nation's future.

In the years before the war, the United States had grown prosperous, productive—and deeply divided. Southern states threatened to leave the Union if their rights under the Constitution were violated. Their leaders cherished a rural way of life that used African-American slaves to raise cotton and tobacco on large plantations. In the North, farmers grew corn and wheat on small, family plots. Northern cities bustled with commerce. On street corners, abolitionists preached the evils of slavery. The South felt besieged and talked of secession. The North vowed to fight any attempt to divide the nation.

When war came, Southerners boasted that each of their soldiers was equal to five Northerners. Given the North's immense resources, their confidence was based on faith, not facts (see the comparison that follows this introduction).

General-in-Chief Winfield Scott designed the Union's Anaconda Plan. As the name implied, it was designed to squeeze the South into submission. At sea, warships blockaded Southern ports and tried to cut off trade. On land, Union forces moved to take control of the Mississippi in an attempt to split the Southern states. That task finished, the Federals stormed into Georgia. To complete the encirclement, the Army of the Potomac set its sights on the Confederate capital at Richmond, Virginia.

The South countered with the Davis Plan, a mixture of diplomacy and armed force. On one front, Southern envoys sailed to Europe to bargain for diplomatic recognition as well as economic and military aid. At home, outnumbered Southern armies prepared to fight a defensive war. Win a few major battles or inflict heavy losses on Union forces, Southern leaders promised, and the North will give up the struggle.

In 1861, the U.S. Army numbered only seventeen thousand regular soldiers, most of whom were stationed in the West. Scott and John Wool, the Army's senior generals, were both in their seventies. The Confederacy, in order to defend its right to exist, had to build an army from scratch. Both sides called for volunteers, and within a matter of days a wave of patriotism swept tens of thousands of new recruits into uniform. In the four years of warfare that followed, some three million men took up arms.

The younger generals who emerged to lead the two armies knew one another's strengths and faults. Most had graduated from the United States Military Academy at West Point, and many had fought in the Mexican War of 1846–1848. When the Civil War broke out, loyalties based on family ties often put former comrades-in-arms on opposing sides. Some rose to the occasion; others faltered. In the brief biographies that follow, you'll meet ten notable Union generals. If you need help in putting Civil War events into their proper order, consult the map and time line on the following pages.

Northern vs. Southern States: a Comparison

CATEGORY	NORTHERN STATES (the Union)	SOUTHERN STATES (the Confederacy)
Population	Over 23,000,000; 4,070,000 men, ages 15–40.	Less than 10,000,000; 1,140,000 men, ages 15–40.
Area	24 states (West Virginia gained statehood in 1863); 670,000 square miles.	11 states; 780,000 square miles.
Manufacturing	110,000 shops and factories.	18,000 shops and factories.
Railroads	22,000 miles of track.	9,000 miles of track.
Major Crops	Corn, wheat, oats.	Cotton, tobacco, rice.
Financial Resources	80% of U.S. bank deposits. Paid for war with paper money backed by gold and silver.	20% of U.S. bank deposits. By war's end, Confederate paper money was nearly worthless.
Soldiers	2,100,000 men served in Union armies during the war.	800,000 men served in Confederate armies during the war.
Warships	90 in 1861; over 700 by war's end. Navy enforced crippling blockade of Southern ports.	0 in 1861. Built or purchased a small fleet of blockade runners and commerce raiders.

Map of the Civil War

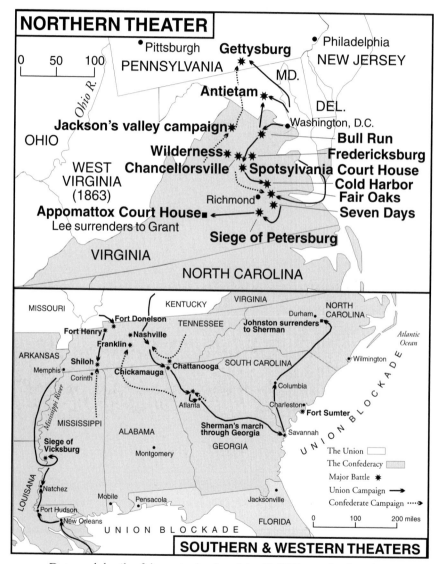

NORTHERN THEATER

0 50 100

•Pittsburgh **Gettysburg** •Philadelphia

PENNSYLVANIA **NEW JERSEY**

Ohio R.

MD.

Antietam✳

DEL.

Jackson's valley campaign✳ •Washington, D.C.

OHIO **Bull Run**

Wilderness✳ **Fredericksburg**

WEST **Chancellorsville** ✳**Spotsylvania Court House**

VIRGINIA **Cold Harbor**

(1863) Richmond•✳ **Fair Oaks**

Appomattox Court House■ ← ✳ **Seven Days**

Lee surrenders to Grant

Siege of Petersburg

VIRGINIA

NORTH CAROLINA

MISSOURI KENTUCKY VIRGINIA NORTH CAROLINA

Durham•

Fort Donelson TENNESSEE **Johnston surrenders**
to Sherman

Fort Henry✳ *Atlantic Ocean*

✳**Nashville**

Franklin✳

ARKANSAS

Shiloh ✳**Chattanooga** SOUTH CAROLINA •Wilmington

Memphis• Corinth **Chickamauga**

Columbia

Atlanta Charleston•

MISSISSIPPI ✳**Fort Sumter**

ALABAMA **Sherman's march**
through Georgia Savannah

Siege of GEORGIA
Vicksburg Montgomery

Mississippi River

The Union
The Confederacy
Major Battle ✳
Union Campaign →
Confederate Campaign ····▶

LOUISIANA

Natchez

Mobile Pensacola Jacksonville

Port Hudson

New Orleans FLORIDA

0 100 200 miles

U N I O N   B L O C K A D E

SOUTHERN & WESTERN THEATERS

Dates and details of the major battles of the Civil War can be found in
the "Time Line: Major Events of the Civil War" on the following pages.

TIME LINE:
Major Events of the Civil War

1820—*Missouri Compromise* balances the number of free and slave states; divides the west into free and slave territories at 36°30′.

1850—*Compromise of 1850* admits California as a free state; allows Utah and New Mexico to exercise popular sovereignty.

1854—*Kansas-Nebraska Bill* allows slavery north of 36°30′.

1856-1859—*Bleeding Kansas*: Proslavery and antislavery forces fight for the right to control Kansas.

1856—Rise of the antislavery Republican Party.

1857—Supreme Court's *Dred Scott* decision strikes down Missouri Compromise; declares that Congress cannot limit spread of slavery.

1859—*John Brown* raids federal arsenal at Harpers Ferry, Virginia. His plan to start a slave revolt fails.

1860—Lincoln elected president. South Carolina secedes from the Union.

1861—Southern states form Confederate States of America (CSA). Confederate troops fire on Fort Sumter in South Carolina (April 12–14).

First Battle of Bull Run (Virginia): Confederates drive back advancing Union forces (July 21).

1862—Union takes forts Henry and Donelson on Tennessee River (February 6–16).

Battle of Shiloh (Tennessee): Confederates win first day, but Union counterattack carries the decisive second day (April 6–7). Union naval forces capture New Orleans (April 25).

Jackson's Valley Campaign (Virginia): General Thomas "Stonewall" Jackson leads Confederate troops to a series of victories in the Shenandoah Valley (May 4–June 9).

Fair Oaks (Virginia): Union forces drive back the Confederates (May 31–June 1).

Seven Days (Virginia): Union forces threaten Richmond before being driven back by General Robert E. Lee (June 25–July 1).

Second Battle of Bull Run (Virginia): Another Southern victory helps the Confederacy regain most of Virginia (August 27–30).

Battle of Antietam (Maryland): Union army holds Lee's forces to a draw in bloodiest day of the war (September 17).

Battle of Fredericksburg (Virginia): Lee soundly defeats Union army led by General Ambrose Burnside (December 13).

1863—Lincoln's *Emancipation Proclamation* frees Southern slaves (Jan. 1).

Battle of Chancellorsville (Virginia): Southern victory marred by death of Stonewall Jackson (May 1–4).

Battle of Gettysburg (Pennsylvania): Greatest battle of the Civil War ends in defeat for Lee and his Southern troops (July 1–3).

Battle of Vicksburg (Mississippi): Confederate garrison surrenders after six-week siege, leaving entire Mississippi in Union hands (May 19–July 4).

Chickamauga (Georgia): Southern victory keeps Northern forces contained in Chattanooga (September 19–20).

Chattanooga campaign (Tennessee): Union victories at Lookout Mountain and Missionary Ridge open way into Georgia (November 23–25).

1864—*Battle of the Wilderness* (Virginia): Lee's victory does not stop General U. S. Grant from advancing on Petersburg and Richmond (May 5–6).

Spotsylvania Court House (Virginia): Another victory for Grant and his Northern forces (May 8–19).

Cold Harbor (Virginia): Lee's Southerners repulse Grant's assault, but the Northerners soon return to the offensive (June 1–3).

Siege of Petersburg (Virginia): Grant and Lee's forces battle for months; the North gradually wears down the outnumbered defenders (June 20, 1864–April 2, 1865).

Battle of Atlanta (Georgia): General William Sherman lays siege to Atlanta (July 17); the city falls on December 21.

March to the Sea: Sherman's troops cut a 40-mile wide swath as they advance to the Atlantic coast (November 16, 1864–February 18, 1865).

Franklin (Tennessee): Confederate troops led by General John Bell Hood are defeated and fail to cut Sherman's supply lines (November 30).

Nashville (Tennessee): Northern victory virtually ends the war in the west (December 15–16).

1865—Richmond falls to Grant's advancing army (April 3).

Appomattox Court House (Virginia): Lee surrenders to Grant (April 9).

Lincoln is shot by John Wilkes Booth (April 14).

North Carolina: Sherman accepts General Joe Johnston's surrender of the last major Southern army (April 26).

General Ambrose Everett Burnside

Ambrose Everett Burnside
(1824–1881)

In August 1849, Lieutenant Ambrose Burnside commanded a lonely army post in New Mexico. After Apaches ambushed a mail shipment, he and his men tracked down a second raiding party. The cavalry soldiers drew their swords and charged the Apaches. Their muzzle-loading rifles were useless in close combat, and they had not been issued pistols. Despite their lack of firepower, the troops won the hard-fought skirmish.

Burnside was sure he could design a better cavalry weapon. In 1853 he resigned from the army and moved to Rhode Island. There he raised some money and began to produce a breech-loading carbine. It was a simple, well-made weapon, capable of rapid fire without overheating. The army bought a few hundred, and hunters snapped up the rest.

In 1857, Secretary of War John Floyd promised Burnside a $90,000 order if the rifles held up in testing. Twice, the carbines beat all rivals. Then Floyd abruptly withdrew his offer. Burnside, it seems, had refused to pay a bribe to one of Floyd's friends.[1]

Burnside sold his sword and uniform to raise cash. Then he assigned all of his assets to his investors and headed west to look for work. A man of honor he believed, should pay off his debts.

Early Life

Ambrose Everett Burnside was born May 23, 1824, in Liberty, Indiana. He was the fourth of nine children of Edghill and Pamela Burnside. Edghill was a well-liked clerk of the county court, but he was poorly paid. As a boy, Ambrose had to help out on the family farm. During the winters, he attended a one-room schoolhouse. A Quaker teacher taught him honesty and kindness, as well as the three R's.

When he was sixteen, Ambrose was apprenticed to a tailor. Two years later, he and a partner opened a shop of their own in Liberty. Edghill was serving a term in the state legislature that year. He used his influence to obtain an appointment to the United States Military Academy for his son. Ambrose was happy to escape the drudgery of the tailor shop.

The young cadet disliked West Point's rigid discipline. During his first year he picked up 198 demerits. Two more would have meant expulsion. Somehow Burnside held on, and graduated in the middle of his class in 1847. The army assigned him to garrison duty in Mexico. His next posting took him to New Mexico, where he escorted the mail and fought Apaches. Bored by frontier life, he sometimes gambled too much.

Burnside married Mary Bishop in 1852. The young officer stood an imposing six feet tall, with brown hair and hazel eyes. He took pride in his mustache, which flowed back to join the hair along the sides of his face. Other men copied the style, which became known as burnsides or sideburns.

After his business failure, Burnside moved to Chicago. George McClellan, a friend from West Point, hired him as cashier for the Illinois Central Railroad. By 1860, Burnside had worked his way up to the post of treasurer in the New York office. He used his handsome salary to pay off his debts.

The Civil War

The South's efforts to break up the Union angered Burnside. When the war broke out, he organized the First Rhode Island Infantry and marched it to Washington. The unit was one of the first to reach the capital. At the First Battle of Bull Run in northern Virginia, his brigade fought well for a time. Then it was caught up in the panic that seized the Union troops in their first real test of the war.

15

In August, Burnside received the star of a brigadier general of volunteers. He led an expedition that seized a stretch of the North Carolina coast and gave the North a much-needed success. The campaign earned him a second star. At Antietam in Maryland, in September 1862, the new major general commanded the left wing of General George McClellan's Army of the Potomac. Ordered to attack General Robert E. Lee's weak right flank, Burnside moved much too slowly. A Confederate counterattack drove him back and opened the way for Lee to withdraw a day later.

McClellan drew the blame for allowing Lee to escape. Badly in need of a fighting general, Lincoln asked Burnside to lead the Army of the Potomac. Burnside knew himself all too well. He told Lincoln he was the wrong man for the job. In the end, he gave in to the urgings of his fellow generals. They preferred the good-natured Burnside to the boastful Joseph Hooker.

Burnside took command on November 7, 1862. At the time, the Confederate army was split. Lee was at Fredericksburg, Virginia, and Stonewall Jackson was campaigning with his men through the Shenandoah Valley. Burnside believed that his job was to carry the fight to Lee. First, he reorganized his army into three grand corps. Then he ordered an attack on Fredericksburg.

The army's advance units reached the Rappahannock River on November 17. Even though the crossings were unguarded, Burnside waited for his pontoon bridges to arrive. Poor staff work back in Washington held them up. As the days slipped past, General James Longstreet's corps arrived to reinforce Lee's army.

At last, on December 11, Union engineers moved six pontoon bridges into the half-frozen river. Each time they pushed a section forward, Southern marksmen opened fire. Many of the well-aimed bullets found their mark. Union riflemen tried to silence the snipers, but without success. A fierce artillery barrage finally silenced the defenders, and Burnside's army marched across the makeshift bridges. On the Union left, General William Franklin's Union troops attacked Prospect Heights, but were thrown back.

On the right, across open fields, lay Marye's Heights. Waves of Bluecoats surged forward, only to be cut down by Confederate riflemen firing from behind a stone wall. Burnside ordered assault after suicidal assault. Union dead piled up in front of the stone wall and sunken road below Marye's Heights. More than one hundred thousand Union troops took part in the battle. When Burnside at last gave the order to break off the attack, more than twelve thousand men lay dead or wounded.

That night, Burnside announced that he would lead the Ninth Corps in a new assault the next day. This time, his generals talked him out of his folly. For two days the armies held their positions. Then, on the night of December 15, the beaten

Union troops commanded by Ambrose Burnside watch as their big guns pound Fredericksburg. The barrage drove Southern snipers out of the town, but Lee's main force lay waiting in the hills beyond. The series of reckless frontal assaults on those positions that Burnside ordered failed to dislodge the Confederate defenders.

Union troops recrossed the river. In a letter to General-in-Chief Henry Halleck, Burnside wrote: "For the failure in the attack, I am responsible, as the extreme gallantry [of the troops] . . . would have carried the points had it been possible."[2]

In mid-January, Burnside found that his luck still ran bad. His new plan called for his army to outflank Lee's forces, but heavy rains turned the roads into quagmires. Reporters who slogged along with the army called it "the Mud March." An officer surveyed the dismal scene and sent a message to headquarters. The note asked for "50 men, 25 feet high, to work in mud 18 feet deep."[3]

Burnside now began to think that his generals were plotting against him. He wrote an order that fired four generals and relieved five others of their commands. On January 24, 1863, he told President Lincoln that he could not carry on unless the order was confirmed. Lincoln realized that his commander was in over his head. He called in "Fighting Joe" Hooker to replace Burnside.

Instead of sending Burnside home, Lincoln put him in command of the Army of the Ohio. Freed of the weight of total command, Burnside performed ably in his new post. Congress passed a resolution that praised him and his men for their service to the nation.

In the spring of 1864, Burnside returned east to take command of the Ninth Corps. The corps, which included seven African-American regiments, fought well during U. S. Grant's advance on Richmond. Lee surrendered on April 9, 1865. Burnside resigned from the army six days later.

Burnside's Legacy

The people of Rhode Island welcomed Burnside home as a war hero. In 1866, the voters elected him governor by an amazing three-to-one majority. Governing the small state was only a part-time job. Burnside spent the rest of his time working for the railroads. After winning two more one-year terms, he returned to private life.

In 1872, the United States Treasury sent Burnside a $37,000 bill for shortfalls in his wartime accounts. To make matters worse, his investments went sour. Beset by money problems, he welcomed the Rhode Island legislature's offer to serve as one of the state's United States senators. He held his seat in Congress from 1874 until his death on September 13, 1881.

Ambrose Burnside was a hard worker, and he looked splendid in his uniform. Friends spoke warmly of his winning smile and noble character. As a general, he fell far short of giants like Lee and Grant. A Rhode Island woman summed him up in these words: "I know there is nothing weighty behind that grand manner," she said, "but what a treasure he is, after all."[4]

Ulysses S. Grant
(1822–1885)

In March 1864, the Civil War was going badly for the North. President Lincoln had tired of generals who promised victories but seldom delivered them. He called on Ulysses S. Grant to serve as the army's general-in-chief.

Two months later, Grant led the Army of the Potomac toward Richmond. The gruff westerner unbent enough to joke with a reporter. "I will agree to be there in about four days," said Grant, "that is, if General Lee becomes a party to the agreement, but if he objects, the trip will doubtedly take longer."[1]

On May 5–7, Grant's troops met Lee's Army of Northern Virginia in a tangle of undergrowth known as the Wilderness. Both sides suffered heavy casualties. Grant lost more than seventeen thousand men

General Ulysses Simpson Grant

killed and wounded (out of 101,000). Lee's smaller army lost 7,750 men, but the Southerners stood firm. Once again, a Union army was forced to pull back.

The pullback did not turn into the retreat everyone expected. Grant quickly turned his army south toward Richmond. Grizzled veterans cheered their commander and marched with a new spring in their step. Two days later, on May 9, they hit the Southerners again. U. S. Grant was dead set on breaking Lee's army, no matter what the cost.

Early Life

Hiram Ulysses Grant was born at Point Pleasant, Ohio, on April 27, 1822. The oldest of six children, "Lyss" grew up on a farm in nearby Georgetown. His father, Jesse, also owned a tannery. Young Lyss hated the tannery, but loved any work that involved horses. Because he disliked the name Hiram, he told people it was his middle name.

Lyss was seventeen when he received an appointment to the United States Military Academy. The congressman who filled out the paperwork wrote the applicant's middle name as Simpson (his mother's maiden name). Grant soon learned to like his new initials. His classmates called blue-eyed, brown-haired U. S. Grant by the nickname "Uncle Sam"—Sam for short.

He was only an average student, but Grant earned a modest fame as West Point's best horseman.

He gentled the academy's wildest horses and jumped the highest fences. In 1843, after graduating near the middle of his class, Lieutenant Grant was stationed near St. Louis. There he courted and married pretty Julia Dent. The marriage produced three boys and a girl.

Grant's courage and drive impressed his commanders during the Mexican War. In 1852 he was transferred to the Pacific Northwest, where he spent two unhappy years. Homesick for his family, he sometimes drank too much. The regiment's commander saw him tipsy one day and threatened a court-martial. Grant resigned in 1854, just as the army promoted him to captain.

Julia's father gave the young couple an eighty-acre farm. Grant worked hard, but failed as a farmer. He then sold real estate, but struck out as a salesman, too. Next, a younger brother gave Grant a job in his leather business. When the Civil War broke out in April 1861, Sam Grant was thirty-nine. His family thought of him as a failure.

The Civil War

Julia's father owned slaves, but Grant thought slavery was wrong. When his country issued a call for soldiers, he stepped forward. Soon he was back in uniform, drilling a ragtag band of volunteers. The need for trained officers was great, and the governor of Illinois gave Grant the rank of colonel. His men called him "the little 'un,'" but learned to respect him. Grant was not a big man, but his steely gaze cowed even the roughest backwoodsmen.

Given command of "Yates's Hellions," Grant soon whipped the rowdy regiment into shape. In September, newly promoted to brigadier general, Grant set up camp at Cairo, Illinois. Two days later he led his troops into Kentucky and captured Paducah, a key river town.

In February 1862, Grant crossed into Tennessee and won two major battles. His 20,000 troops, backed up by navy gunboats, attacked the Southern strong points at Fort Henry and Fort Donelson. At Fort Donelson, the officer in charge agreed to surrender but asked to bargain over the terms. Grant wrote back, "No terms except an unconditional and immediate surrender can be accepted."[2] The press hailed the new hero and said his initials stood for "Unconditional Surrender" Grant. Lincoln promoted him to major general.

The fall of the forts opened the way for a Union effort to cut the South in two. In April, Grant struck the first blow. At the bloodbath known as the Battle of Shiloh, his troops pushed Southern forces south into Mississippi. Before the battle, Grant injured himself in a fall from his horse. Back in Washington, rumors flew that he had been drinking again. The president held firm when critics said that Grant should be fired. "I can't spare this man—he fights," Lincoln said.[3]

In 1863, Grant proved Lincoln right by mounting a brilliant campaign against Vicksburg. The city was the South's last stronghold on the Mississippi. Grant took a huge risk by cutting his army loose from its supply lines and bypassing the city. In early May, he sent troops eastward to Jackson, where they defeated General Joe Johnston's Confederate forces. Then he turned west to lay siege to Vicksburg. The city surrendered on July 4 after holding out for seven hellish weeks. A staff officer wrote, "When the time came to risk all, he went in like a . . . hero, whom no ill omens could deject and no triumph unduly exalt."[4]

The victory vaulted Grant into command of all western armies. He moved northward quickly to relieve the Union forces trapped at Chattanooga, Tennessee. In November, his men won major battles at Lookout Mountain and Missionary Ridge. Southern forces fled into Georgia, opening the way for General William Sherman's "March to the Sea."

Farther east, Lee's army still blocked the way to Richmond, the Confederate capital. Lincoln summoned Grant to take command of all Union forces. Now a lieutenant general, Grant could have directed the war from his desk in Washington. When the Army of the Potomac crossed into Virginia in May 1864, however, Grant rode with his men. The South's General James Longstreet knew that the war had taken a deadly turn. He warned, "That man will fight us every day and every hour until the end of the war."[5]

Grant headed toward Richmond because that was where Lee's Army of Northern Virginia lay waiting. To defeat the South, he had to beat the canny "Bobbie" Lee. As Union casualties soared at the battles of the Wilderness, Spotsylvania, and Cold Harbor, critics began calling him "Butcher Grant." Grant shook off the complaints. "I propose to fight it out on this line if it takes all summer," he announced.[6]

Lee and Grant were well matched. Time after time Grant sidestepped southward, only to find Lee's tattered army standing in the way. As the summer wore on, Grant managed to pin the Southern forces into siege lines that ran from Petersburg to Richmond. At long last, he had deprived Lee of his ability to maneuver. In the deep South, Sherman's army captured Atlanta, Georgia. After pausing to regroup, he sent his troops rampaging toward Savannah.

In April of 1865, the Southern lines outside Richmond broke. As Lee's shattered army pulled back, Grant kept up the pressure. At last, the hungry, barefoot Southerners could fight no more. Lee met with Grant at Appomattox Court House to discuss the terms of surrender. Lee wore his best uniform to the meeting. Grant showed up dressed in a rumpled private's coat, his stars pinned to the shoulder straps.

Despite his nickname, Grant did not demand unconditional surrender. Though he lacked the authority to do so, he offered generous terms. If Southern troops would lay down their arms, he said,

After stretching Lee's lines until they finally broke, Grant's Union troops flooded into the capital of the Confederacy. By the time they entered the city, Richmond lay in ruins. During their retreat, Confederate troops set fires that destroyed more than 900 buildings and damaged hundreds more.

they would be free to go home to their families. He even allowed Confederate officers to keep their side arms and horses. Grant had taken an important first step toward healing the nation's wounds.

Grant's Legacy

General William Sherman once summed up Grant's strengths. "I'll tell you where he beats me and where he beats the world," Sherman said. "He don't care a damn for what the enemy does out of his sight, but it scares me like hell. . . . He issues his orders and does his level best to carry them out without much reference to what is going on about him."[7]

In 1868, the Republican party picked the war hero to run for president. Grant won and served two terms, but he was ill-equipped for the job. Untrained in the ways of politics, he put too much trust in the scoundrels who surrounded him. Scandals tarred his administration. To make matters worse, Grant believed that presidents should not oppose the will of Congress. When radical Republicans passed harsh laws that punished the South, he did not interfere.

After leaving office in 1877, Grant toured Europe for two years. He invested his money with his son, but the firm went bankrupt. Ailing and in debt, Grant began writing his life story. Racked by the pain of his throat cancer, he died on July 23, 1885, a week after he finished his manuscript. Rushed into print by his publisher, the humorist Mark Twain, the memoirs became a runaway bestseller.

General Henry Wager Halleck

Henry Wager Halleck
(1815–1872)

You loved him or hated him. Nobody seemed to be neutral on the subject of General Henry Halleck.

Friends knew him as "Old Brains," a tribute to his keen mind. Behind his back, critics called him "Old Wooden Head." This nickname paid tribute to Halleck's stubbornness. President Lincoln wrote him off as "little more than a first rate file clerk."

Halleck was a "desk soldier" at a time when the Union needed inspiring leaders. General George McClellan called Halleck "the most hopelessly stupid of all men in high position." Secretary of the Navy Gideon Welles agreed. Welles said that Halleck "takes no responsibility, plans nothing, suggests nothing, is good for nothing."[1]

On the plus side, Halleck was a fine organizer. When he took charge, supplies arrived on time. This behind-the-scenes work doesn't win headlines, however. The general's looks and manner also repelled people. One author sums up Halleck as "pop-eyed, flabby, surly, and crafty . . . the most unpopular man in Washington. [Even though he was incompetent] in matters of strategy and leadership, Halleck played a major role in the administration of the Civil War."[2]

Early Life

Henry Wager Halleck was born on January 16, 1815 in the Mohawk Valley town of Westerville, New York. The baby was the first of thirteen children born to Joseph and Catherine Halleck. At sixteen, Henry ran away from the family farm to live with his Grandfather Wager. The older man took the bright teenager under his wing and helped him catch up on his schooling. When Henry was twenty, Wager helped him win a place at the United States Military Academy. Halleck was a brilliant student and graduated third in the class of 1839.

The new second lieutenant taught French at West Point for a year. Transferred to New York, he worked to upgrade the city's defenses. In 1844, the army sent Halleck to France to study. On his return, he gave a series of lectures that was published as *Elements of Military Art and Science.* The widely read book argued that wars are won by attacking key cities and cutting supply routes.

During the Mexican War, Halleck was stationed on the West Coast. He saw almost no fighting, except for one attack on an outlying ranch. The army found a better use for his talents when it came to governing California. Halleck played a leading role in writing the state-to-be's constitution. By the end of the war, he had risen to the rank of captain.

In 1849, Halleck helped open a law office. Halleck, Peachy, and Billings soon became one of the leading firms in the state. Content with his new life, Halleck retired from the army in 1854. A year later he married Elizabeth Hamilton, granddaughter of Alexander Hamilton. When the Civil War erupted in 1861, Halleck was active in railroading and mining. He was well on his way to becoming a millionaire.

The Civil War

In 1861, the North needed proven officers. General-in-Chief Winfield Scott thought of Henry Halleck and the textbook he had written. Scott asked President Lincoln to appoint Halleck to the rank of major general. Some thought Scott was grooming Halleck to replace him. At forty-six, Halleck looked more like a balding shopkeeper than a military hero. He carried 190 pounds on a five foot nine inch frame. The loose skin on his face seemed to quiver when he talked. His eyes seldom met those of the men he commanded.[3]

The army sent Halleck to take command of the Department of the Missouri. He reached St. Louis in

November 1861 and quickly brought order to the chaos left by John Charles Frémont. In December, Halleck turned his attention to Missouri's guerrilla bands. After his men swept the guerrillas aside, he took aim at General Sterling Price's regular Confederate forces.

Halleck's field commanders made him look like a genius. In February 1862, General U. S. Grant won victories at Fort Henry on the Tennessee River and Fort Donelson on the Cumberland. In March, General Samuel Curtis defeated Price at Pea Ridge, Arkansas. This victory removed a Confederate threat to southwest Missouri. That same month, General John Pope cleared Southern forces from Island No. 10. The strongpoint had played havoc with Union gunboats on the Mississippi.

Halleck basked in the reflected glory of these triumphs. Soon he was lobbying for the overall command of Union troops in the West. To increase his prestige, he asked Washington to send him fifty thousand additional soldiers. His request was turned down, but on March 8, Halleck assumed command of the new Department of the Mississippi. The huge department included most of the area west of the Allegheny Mountains. "Old Brains" now was a key player in the Union war effort.

True to his textbook, Halleck looked on war as a chess match. The board for this game was the Mississippi Valley. The Confederate army led by Joe Johnston was the South's queen. Defeat that force,

and the South's king—the river port of Vicksburg—
would fall into his hands. Halleck opened the match
by ordering Grant to advance on Johnston's base at
the rail center of Corinth, Mississippi. In April, after
his bloody victory at Shiloh, Tennessee, Grant
resumed his march toward Corinth. Halleck hurried
to the scene to take command.

Once he was in the field, "Old Brains" seemed to
lose his nerve. Instead of moving swiftly to destroy
Johnston's army, he set his sights on Corinth. He
advanced at a snail's pace, digging in each night to
repel a surprise attack that never came. Early in May,
his forces drove to within a few miles of the city.
Then, instead of seeking battle, Halleck ordered his
men to set up siege lines. The delay gave Johnston
time to withdraw. The Southerners further delayed
pursuit by leaving their lines "manned" by dummy
soldiers and log "cannon." Two weeks later, Halleck
called off the game. He had won a few pawns but had
failed to capture the foe's queen.

In July 1862, Lincoln called Halleck back to
Washington to become the new general-in-chief. The
job called for someone with management skills, and
that was Halleck's strength. Later, Lincoln had good
reason to regret his choice. As one critic puts it,
"Unable to command successfully one army,
[Halleck] was ordered to Washington to command
all the armies."[4]

Halleck did some splendid work in one critical
area. In his new post he made sure the troops had the

weapons and supplies they needed. Confusion gave way to efficiency, rules, and coordination. In the turmoil of wartime Washington, "Old Brains" reveled in the capital's intrigue and excitement. His achievements were real, but he made few friends. To hear him tell it, he was never wrong. His staff had to take the blame when he made any of his many mistakes.[5]

Field generals soon wearied of the telegrams their deskbound commander fired their way. Slow-moving General William Rosecrans was a favorite target. As Rosecrans dawdled in Murfreesboro, Tennessee, Halleck's telegrams urged him to strike. "Old Rosy" held firm, content to build up his forces. Halleck was driven to complain that the daily exchange of telegrams was straining the army's budget. When Rosecrans moved at last, his men drove the Confederates back to Chattanooga.

As the months dragged on, Lincoln saw that Halleck could organize an army, but couldn't lead it. In March 1864, he gave the job to U. S. Grant, a man who could lead. Demoted to chief of staff, Halleck stayed at his desk. He was still serving there when the war ended a year later.

Halleck's Legacy

Lincoln's death gave Secretary of War Edwin Stanton a chance to move Halleck out of Washington. He sent the former general-in-chief to Richmond to serve as commander of the Military District of the James. Halleck's attempts to help Southerners get

One of Henry Halleck's jobs was to keep a constant flow of armaments moving to the front lines. This Union railroad mortar, nicknamed "Dictator," hurled 400-pound shells into Petersburg during the siege of 1864. When its crew first fired the mortar, the support beams buckled under the shock.

back on their feet earned him few thanks in the North. Advising freed slaves to go back to the plantations drew cries of outrage. Halleck next sold army horses to local farmers and hired a Richmond ironworks to repair weapons. These attempts to rebuild the shattered region drew sharp protests from Washington.

By August, Stanton was convinced that "Old Brains" was a "great scoundrel." He sent the general to San Francisco to take command of the Pacific District. The home folks did not give Halleck the parades and parties other war heroes received. Somehow, he had emerged from the war as a villain, not a hero. He looked old beyond his fifty years.

As the months went by, Union generals began to publish their memoirs. Almost to a man, fairly or unfairly, they took dead aim at Halleck. His faults were magnified and his strengths were ignored. In 1869, the army moved him to the Division of the South. It was his final command. Henry Wager Halleck died in Louisville on January 9, 1872.

Winfield Scott Hancock
(1824–1886)

May 12, 1864 dawned cold and wet. General Winfield Hancock was moving his Second Corps into place for an assault on the Southern lines near Spotsylvania, Virginia. At 4:35 the fog lifted slightly and Hancock gave the signal to advance. The twenty thousand men moved forward in a silent mass. Ahead lay twelve hundred yards of pine groves and a strong Confederate force. As the Bluecoats neared the Southern trenches, they yelled and broke into a run.

The attackers scaled a barricade and stormed into the Southern lines. Men fought hand to hand with bayonets and rifle butts. Within minutes Hancock's troops had overrun a mile of trenches. The Southern cannon fell into the hands of oncoming Northerners

General Winfield Scott Hancock

before their crews could fire a shot. Some of the defenders fled, but twenty-eight hundred Southerners laid down their arms.

The prisoners included two Southern generals. One was Hancock's prewar friend, Edwin "Old Allegheny" Johnson. When Johnson saw Hancock, he threw his arms around the younger general. With tears in his eyes, Johnson said, "This is damned bad luck, yet I would rather have had this good fortune to fall to you than to any other man living."[1] Hancock inspired that kind of respect in all who knew him.

Early Life

Winfield Scott Hancock and his twin brother Hilary were born February 4, 1824 in southeastern Pennsylvania. Winfield was named for General Winfield Scott, hero of the War of 1812. When the boys were two, the family moved to Norristown. Elizabeth Hancock, their mother, ran a ladies' hat shop in their home. Two years later, Benjamin, their father, gave up teaching and took up the practice of law.

The twins started school at the Norristown Academy. To save money, Benjamin later transferred them to a free public school. Young Winfield combined a love of good times with a quick, clever mind. In 1840, a lawyer friend helped him win an appointment to the United States Military Academy. Hilary stayed home and studied law.

Winfield was sixteen when he reached West Point. Over the next four years, he grew nine inches, topping out at a robust six feet two inches. His fellow cadets described him as handsome, graceful, and manly. He had a kind word for everyone, but he could curse like a muleskinner. At graduation in 1844, Hancock ranked in the bottom third of his class.

The new officer began his army career with a tour of duty in Indian Territory. During the Mexican War, he won a promotion for gallantry in action. Six years of peacetime service ended in 1856, when Hancock joined a campaign to subdue the Seminoles. A year later, he rode with the troops sent to pacify Utah during the bloodless Mormon War.

In 1850, Hancock had married Almira Russell in St. Louis. In 1859, he took his wife and two children with him to his new post in California. The family enjoyed its stay in Los Angeles, then a sleepy town of four thousand. When the Civil War broke out in 1861, Captain Hancock cast his lot with the Union.

The Civil War

Hancock won his first victory before he left Los Angeles. The show of force he staged frightened local Southerners and helped keep California in the Union. When he reached Washington, he was promoted to brigadier general. With the new rank came command of a brigade in the Army of the Potomac.

The 1862 Peninsula campaign proved Hancock's worth. After his brigade routed a Southern force at

Troops who marched into battle with Winfield Scott Hancock could expect to see heavy fighting. This soldier from the 8th Pennsylvania Volunteers proudly displays the tattered battle flag that he and his comrades carried through some of the most ferocious fighting of the war.

Williamsburg, Virginia, General George McClellan sent a wire to Washington. "Hancock was superb!" the message read. From that day on, news reports often referred to Hancock "the Superb."[2]

In September 1862, Hancock took command of First Division, Second Corps while the battle of Antietam (Maryland) raged around him. His troops held firm in the center of the line, but the heaviest fighting was over. A promotion to major general came in time for Hancock to command the Second Corps at Fredericksburg, Virginia. His brigades fought bravely, pushing to within forty yards of the Southern lines below Marye's Heights. At that point, deadly Confederate fire drove them back. After the Union defeat at Chancellorsville, Virginia, in May 1863, Hancock fought a brilliant rearguard action. His skirmish lines held off the pursuing Southerners and allowed the battered Union army to escape.

On June 28, 1863, General George Meade took command of the Army of the Potomac. On July 1, Meade heard that a battle was shaping up near the town of Gettysburg, Pennsylvania. After learning that General John Reynolds had been killed there, Meade sent Hancock to take charge of the Union forces. Neither side knew it, but one of the war's key battles was about to begin.

Hancock reached Gettysburg about 4:00 P.M. Riding to the crest of Cemetery Ridge, he surveyed the scene. With his usual quick judgment, he announced, "I select this as the battlefield."[3] His next job was to restore order to troops who were close to panic. The sight of Hancock calmly preparing for battle seemed to do the job. Moving swiftly, he began to organize a mile-long defensive line that stretched from Culp's Hill to the Round Tops. The Confederate assault he had expected did not come that day. As dusk fell, Union reinforcements came streaming in. Meade arrived and assumed command.

On July 2, Hancock and his corps held the Union center. He watched amazed as Union general Daniel Sickles ordered his troops to occupy a nearby ridge. The ill-timed maneuver exposed the Union left flank. When the Southern attack came, Sickles was wounded and his corps was driven back. Hancock called in fresh troops and counterattacked. His determined assault reclaimed the lost ground near Little Round Top.

General Robert E. Lee ignored protests from his staff and ordered an attack on the Union center. On July 3, the assault began with an artillery barrage. Hancock had just finished lunch when one of the first shells blew the table to splinters. To steady his troops, Hancock rode along the ridge, fully exposed to enemy fire. When told that a general should not risk his life, Hancock replied, "There are times when a corps commander's life does not matter."[4]

From the Southern lines, fifteen thousand Confederate troops advanced toward him in perfect ranks. Hancock steadied his men as the long gray line swept forward. When the firing began, he rode back and forth, alert for problems. Spotting a weakness near the center of the line, he called for troops to fill the gap. As they did so, a bullet smashed Hancock's saddle and ripped into his inner thigh. The slug carried with it bits of wood and a bent saddle nail. Two officers caught the general as he fell. One of them stopped the bleeding with a tourniquet made from a handkerchief and a pistol barrel. Despite the pain, Hancock waited until the Southerners fell back before he allowed his men to carry him to the rear.

The painful wound kept Hancock out of action for six months. By year's end he was well enough to join General U. S. Grant's advance into Virginia. His Second Corps performed nobly at the battles of the Wilderness, Spotsylvania, Cold Harbor, and Petersburg. When his wound flared up in November 1864, Grant sent him back to Washington.

Hancock's new job was to recruit former soldiers to serve as sentries, nurses, and cooks. The war-weary veterans did not respond well to the idea. Hancock then moved on to command the Department of West Virginia. He was serving there when the Southern armies laid down their arms.

Hancock's Legacy

In war or peace, Hancock was a career army man. A major general in the regular army, he served briefly on the western plains after the war ended. In 1867, he led the Seventh Cavalry on a campaign to pacify the Plains tribes. Instead of bringing peace, he stirred up a small war by burning a Cheyenne village.

After leaving Kansas, Hancock commanded the Departments of Missouri and of Texas and Louisiana. Alarmed by the harshness of the Reconstruction laws, he tried to soften their impact. In November 1867, he issued an order that restored civilian rule to Texas and Louisiana. The order brought Hancock into conflict with Washington and a transfer to less sensitive posts. For the next eighteen years, Hancock commanded several key departments—but none in the South.

In 1880, Hancock returned to center stage. The Democratic party chose the war hero to run for president. The Republicans could not attack his war record, but they argued that he knew little about the art of governing. Speakers pointed to Grant's failed presidency and warned against voting for another general. When the electoral votes were counted, James Garfield won the White House, 214–155. The popular vote was much closer. Garfield collected 4,449,053 votes to Hancock's 4,442,030, a margin of only 7,023 votes.

As the years rolled past, Hancock developed diabetes. His friends knew he was in ill health, but he refused to see a doctor. A boil on his neck turned into a carbuncle. All attempts to heal the painful infection failed. Winfield Scott Hancock died at his Governors Island headquarters on February 9, 1886.

General Joseph Hooker

Joseph Hooker
(1814–1878)

In December 1862, the Army of the Potomac was disheartened by its defeat at Fredericksburg, Virginia. President Lincoln fired General Ambrose Burnside. After a lively debate with his advisers, he picked General Joseph "Fighting Joe" Hooker to lead the army. A month later, Lincoln sent his new commander a most unusual letter: "I think it best for you to know that . . . I am not quite satisfied with you. I think that during General Burnside's command of the Army, you have taken counsel of your ambition, and thwarted him as much as you could, in which you did a great wrong to your country, and to a most . . . honorable brother officer. I have heard . . . of your recently saying that both the Army and the Government needed a dictator. Of course, it was not for this, but in spite of it, that I have given you command. . . . I much fear that the spirit which you have aided to infuse into the Army, of criticizing their Commander, and withholding confidence from him, will now turn upon you."[1]

Lincoln's letter was prophetic. Hooker lasted only a few months in his new command.

Early Life

Joseph Hooker was born November 13, 1814, in Hadley, Massachusetts. He was the fourth child and only son of Joseph and Mary Hooker. After his father's business failed, young Joe knew what it was like to be poor. When Hopkins Academy began charging twelve dollars a year, the Hookers could not afford the fees. Joe earned the money himself by assembling wire-and-wood devices used to spin wool.

The boy set his sights on the United States Military Academy, where tuition was free. A friendly teacher helped him win the appointment in 1833. The tall, wavy-haired eighteen-year-old was popular with his classmates. He was less so with his teachers. When he graduated in 1837, Hooker ranked near the middle of his class.

Second Lieutenant Hooker saw service in Florida during the Seminole War. During the Mexican War, he fought with the forces that invaded Mexico. He emerged in 1848 with a well-earned reputation for courage. His battlefield heroics earned him three quick steps up in rank.

In 1849, Lieutenant Colonel Hooker was posted to Sonoma, California. Bored by peacetime duties, he spent his free hours drinking and gambling at the Blue Wing Tavern. In 1851, he took a two-year leave of absence to try his hand at farming. He built a house on his 550-acre farm, but his grapevines and potato crops failed.

Hooker resigned from the army in 1853 and entered politics. He won election as a road overseer but lost his run for the California state assembly. Over the next few years, one writer says, "the dashing army officer had descended almost to the level of beachcomber."[2] A job as Oregon's Superintendent of Military Roads kept Hooker going for a while. By the time the Civil War began, he was broke and back in California.

The Civil War

Hooker had always been strongly pro-Union and antislavery. When the Civil War began, he traveled to Washington, D.C., on borrowed money to seek a command. General Winfield Scott, remembering old clashes with the young officer, ignored his requests. In July, Hooker watched the North's defeat at the First Battle of Bull Run, in Virginia, from the sidelines.

After the battle, Hooker showed up at a White House reception. He looked President Lincoln in the eye and said, "I am a . . . better General than you, Sir, had on that field."[3] Lincoln listened, liked what he heard, and offered Hooker the rank of colonel. Congress went a step farther and gave him a brigadier general's star. In August, Hooker took charge of training twelve newly formed brigades.

General George McClellan launched the Peninsula Campaign in April 1862. Hooker's Second Division led the advance on Williamsburg, Virginia. As battle reports flowed back to Washington, headline writers dubbed him "Fighting Joe" Hooker. The nickname stuck, even though Hooker disliked it. In May, he added the second star of a major general. His division, transferred to the First Corps, fought well in the battles of Antietam in Maryland and Fredericksburg in Virginia. He sometimes drank too much, but his men liked Hooker. They knew that he worked hard to keep them well fed and supplied.

At Antietam, a bullet hit Hooker in the foot. McClellan wrote to his officer, "Had you not been wounded when you were, I believe the result of the battle would have been the entire destruction of the rebel army. I know, that with you at its head, the corps would have . . . gained the main road."[4] McClellan may have been using Hooker's wound to excuse his own failure to use his reserves.

Three months later, General Ambrose Burnside replaced McClellan. At Fredericksburg, Burnside ordered futile assaults on the strongest point in the Southern defenses. As dead Bluecoats piled up in front of Marye's Heights, Hooker turned his wrath on his commander. Stung by the criticism, Burnside

Outside Fredericksburg, an eerie peace has descended on the firing pits and stone wall from which Southern riflemen once gunned down thousands of Union troops. After watching his men die in a fruitless effort to storm the wall, "Fighting Joe" Hooker turned his wrath on Ambrose Burnside, the general who ordered the attack.

asked Lincoln to fire Hooker and some other officers. Instead, on January 26, 1863, Lincoln named "Fighting Joe" to replace Burnside. The president did so with reluctance, and said so in his letter to Hooker.

The Army of the Potomac outnumbered Robert E. Lee's Army of Northern Virginia, 134,000 to 60,000. Hooker's plan was to hold Lee at Fredericksburg with a third of his troops. The rest of the army circled westward to attack Lee from the rear. It was a good plan, and Hooker boasted, "[The Southerners] might as well pack up their haversacks and make for Richmond."[5] The Southern cavalry, however, tracked the move. Lee left 10,000 men to hold his lines and advanced on Hooker with the rest of his army. Surprised by the move, Hooker lost his nerve and pulled back his advance units.

Ever the gambler, Lee split his outnumbered army. A force of 17,000 stayed behind to hold Hooker in place. At the same time, Confederate General "Stonewall" Jackson led 26,000 men on a forced march that turned the exposed Union right flank. Jackson's headlong attack on May 2 sent the Union troops reeling back.

Hooker was forced to retreat. On May 3, he suffered a mild concussion when a shell burst nearby. He recovered quickly, but the shock seemed to rob him of the will to fight. As the Northerners pulled into defensive positions, Lee turned on the Union force at Fredericksburg. Hooker held his ground for three days. On May 6, soundly beaten, he withdrew to safety beyond the Rappahannock River. Lincoln had told him to "put in all your men." Instead, Hooker had allowed a third of his army to stand idle.[6]

In June, Lee began his fateful advance into Pennsylvania. Hooker maneuvered his army to keep it between Lee and Washington. When his plan to abandon one of his strong points was turned down, he asked to be relieved. His critics said he welcomed the excuse to avoid another battle with Lee. Lincoln gave the command to General George Meade on June 28. Within the week, Meade won a crushing victory over Lee at Gettysburg.

The army sent Hooker west to take command of the Twentieth Corps. "Fighting Joe" led the corps at Lookout Mountain and Missionary Ridge in Tennessee, and in the siege of Atlanta. Reporters called his easy victory at Lookout Mountain "the Battle above the Clouds." Their stories restored some of Hooker's lost prestige.

During the Atlanta campaign, General Oliver Howard assumed command of the Army of Tennessee. An outraged Hooker argued that he was next in line for the command. He asked to be relieved—and no one disagreed. Washington moved "Fighting Joe" to the quiet Northern District. His combat days were over.

Hooker's Legacy

Joeseph Hooker was called on to perform a sad duty in April 1865. After Lincoln was shot, his body was returned to Springfield, Illinois, for burial. As commander of the Northern District, Hooker led the honor guard at the funeral.

Although he was attractive to women, Hooker had never married. In September 1865, at age fifty, he wed Olivia Groesbeck in Cincinnati. Two months later, at a reception in New York City, the bridegroom suffered a stroke. Months passed before he regained the use of his right arm and leg.

In early 1867, Hooker suffered a second stroke. To aid his recovery, he and Olivia took a trip to Europe. In July 1868, shortly after their return, Olivia died. Hooker retired three months later. Money from his wife's estate allowed him to live his last years in comfort.

Hooker died in Garden City, New York, on October 31, 1878. History remembers him as a fine strategist and an able corps leader. His faults showed most clearly when the stakes were high, in battle or at the card table. Hooker played a fine game of poker, a friend observed, "until it came to the point where he should go a thousand better, and then he would funk."[7]

George B. McClellan
(1826–1885)

In July 1861, General Irvin McDowell drew the blame for the disaster at Bull Run in Virginia. President Lincoln dismissed the luckless McDowell and replaced him with young George B. McClellan. The new leader of the Army of the Potomac relished the newspaper stories that called him "the Young Napoleon." The day after he arrived in the capital, he wrote, "I find myself in a new and strange position here—President, Cabinet, General Scott, and all deferring to me—By some strange . . . magic I seem to have become the power of the land."[1]

McClellan's conceit was enormous. After Lincoln lectured him on strategy, he referred to the president as "a gorilla." A few evenings later, McClellan came home to learn that Lincoln was waiting in his parlor.

General George Brinton McClellan

A porter told him that the president had been there for an hour. McClellan shrugged and went upstairs to his quarters. A short time later, the porter informed Lincoln that the general had gone to bed.

Lincoln was a forgiving man. He allowed McClellan to keep his command. It was "Little Mac's" failures on the battlefield that cost him his job.

Early Life

George Brinton McClellan was born in Philadelphia, Pennsylvania, on December 3, 1826. He was the third child and second son of Dr. George McClellan and his wife, Elizabeth. Young George grew up happy, robust, and full of promise. He spent four years at a local school, then went on to a top prep school. At thirteen he enrolled at the University of Pennsylvania. During his two years there, he earned top marks despite his youth. In 1842, George won an appointment to the United States Military Academy.

The fifteen-year-old was five months under the minimum age for West Point. Officials checked his record, noted his athletic five foot eight inch frame, and waived the rule. McClellan loved the challenge. When he took the written entrance exams in January, only one cadet outscored him. Outside the classroom, his classmates warmed to his friendly, outgoing nature. He enjoyed an active social life and still managed to stand second in the brilliant class of 1846.

McClellan won praise for his road-building skills during the Mexican War. By the end of the war, he had climbed to the rank of captain. After the war, he spent three years at West Point as an instructor. In his free time he designed a saddle that the army adopted for its cavalry units. He also found time to woo and later marry the beautiful Ellen Marcy.

Secretary of War Jefferson Davis took the bright young officer under his wing. After a trip west to map railroad routes, McClellan sailed to Europe to observe a war in the Crimea. The report he wrote on cavalry tactics helped build his reputation. In 1857, he left the army to become chief engineer of the Illinois Central Railroad. Before long he moved up to vice president. In 1860, he switched to the Ohio and Mississippi Railroad as its president. The job paid an astounding ten thousand dollars a year.

The Civil War

The outbreak of the Civil War in April 1861 put McClellan back in uniform. Although he believed in states' rights, he chose to fight for the Union. In his military career he had seen more service as an army engineer than as a combat officer. Despite this, three states—New York, Ohio, and Pennsylvania—offered him command of their volunteers. McClellan chose Ohio. The state's governor awarded him the two stars of a major general of volunteers on April 23.

Ten days later, McClellan transferred to the regular army with the same rank. The army put him in charge of the Department of the Ohio. Clearly, the former captain was a rising star. He now ranked second only to aging General-in-Chief Winfield Scott.

Early in June McClellan's men mounted the Union's first offensive. An army of eleven thousand troops crossed the Ohio River and surged into western Virginia. By mid-July the Bluecoats had driven Southern troops from the northwestern part of the state. McClellan took the lion's share of the credit. Only later did critics point out that junior officers had done most of the fighting. Two years later, the region joined the Union as the state of West Virginia.

On July 21, 1861, poorly trained Union forces broke and ran at Bull Run. The next day, McClellan received the telegram that summoned him to center stage. Lincoln gave him command of the troops gathered near the capital. McClellan soon organized the scattered units into the Army of the Potomac. At age thirty-four, he commanded the North's largest army.

McClellan worked overtime that summer and fall of 1861. He drilled his troops hard, fed them well, and enforced discipline. The drills and discipline restored order and pride to the army. The soldiers called him "Little Mac" and cheered when he said, "I shall . . . crush the rebels in one campaign."[2] McClellan was also sniping at General-in-Chief Scott, who rejected some of his plans. On November 1, Scott resigned, and Lincoln named McClellan as the new general-in-chief.

McClellan had proven his genius as an organizer and planner. Now that it was time to fight, he revealed a fatal flaw. When his staff told him that he was outnumbered, McClellan believed the overblown numbers. His friend Alan Pinkerton, the great detective, backed up the inflated reports. By the time he took the field in the spring, McClellan thought he faced an army of 250,000 men. In fact, the forces blocking his advance numbered closer to 60,000.

As the weeks slipped by, Lincoln pressured McClellan to advance straight at Richmond, Virginia, the Confederate capital. McClellan favored a roundabout route. His plan called for shipping his troops down the Chesapeake Bay. From there he planned a march up the peninsula between the York and the James rivers. Planning stopped in December, when McClellan fell ill with typhoid fever. Late that month, Lincoln's General Order No. 1 called on all Union forces to advance by February 22, 1862. The date came and went. In March, McClellan at last moved his troops to the peninsula.

The long-delayed Peninsular Campaign began on April 4. It ended a day later. A "fighting" general would have ordered an assault on the Confederate lines. McClellan chose to conduct a time-consuming siege. Weeks passed as the Union troops inched forward. To their disgust, they found that some captured strongpoints were armed with "Quaker guns" (logs painted to look like cannon).

By early June, McClellan's troops were nearing Richmond. On June 26, General Robert E. Lee counterattacked. In a series of battles known as the Seven Days, the Confederates kept up a relentless pressure. McClellan retreated, even though his men won most of the battles. By July 3, he had given up, and his army straggled back. "Little Mac" blamed his failure on Washington's refusal to send fresh troops. Lincoln said he had the "slows," and called off the Peninsula Campaign.

General John Pope replaced McClellan—and promptly led the army into a major defeat at the Second Battle of Bull Run. In August, Lincoln again asked "Little Mac" to take command. Then, as Lee advanced into Maryland, his battle plans fell into Union hands. "Here is a paper," a delighted McClellan told his aides, "with which, if I cannot whip Bobbie Lee, I will be willing to go home."[3]

For once, McClellan moved quickly. He met Lee at Antietam Creek in Maryland on September 17. His troops outnumbered Lee's men two to one, but McClellan was his usual fearful self. Given the opportunity to destroy the Southern army, he fought a defensive battle. When Lee pulled back the next day, McClellan refused to pursue him.

Lincoln was furious. In November 1862, he relieved McClellan of his command. "Little Mac" went home to wait for orders that never came. His active military career was over.

In October 1862 President Lincoln (center) visited General George McClellan's camp at Antietam. In this photo, he poses with Allan Pinkerton (left), who ran a spy system behind Confederate lines, and politician-turned-soldier General John McClernand. A month later, Lincoln relieved McClellan of his command for failing to pursue and destroy Lee's crippled army.

McClellan's Legacy

In 1864, the Democrats picked McClellan to run for president against Lincoln and the Republicans. "Little Mac" vowed to carry on the war—but his party stood for "peace at any price." Although antiwar Northerners gave him their votes, McClellan lost badly. The count showed that he carried only three states.

McClellan resigned from the army and traveled abroad from 1864 to 1868. When he returned, he worked as a chief engineer for the city of New York. In 1877, he returned to politics and won election as governor of New Jersey. During his three years in office, he wiped out the state tax, improved the schools, and built up a state militia.

McClellan died of heart problems in Orange, New Jersey, on October 29, 1885. His memoirs, *McClellan's Own Story*, went to press two years later. McClellan used the book to defend himself. History agrees that he could organize and maneuver an army. It also notes that he lacked the "killer instinct." During a battle, "Little Mac" often stayed far behind the lines. He left the fighting to others while he studied maps and begged for more men and more guns.

General George Gordon Meade

George Gordon Meade
(1815–1872)

On the night of July 2, 1863, General George Meade called his officers to a council of war. His Army of the Potomac lay in a fishhook-shaped formation on the east and south of Gettysburg, Pennsylvania. For two days, the Bluecoats had been fighting a stubborn defensive battle. Their valor had stalled Robert E. Lee's invasion of the North.

This was Meade's fifth day as commander of the North's most important army. He turned to General John Gibbon, commander of the Second Corps. "If Lee attacks tomorrow, it will be on your front," Meade said. Asked why he thought so, he replied, "Because he has made attacks on both our flanks and failed. If he concludes to try it again, it will be on our center."[1]

By trusting his intuition, Meade won a place in history. Lee did renew the attack. On July 3, General George Pickett and his Virginians attacked the Union center. The Southerners put on a brilliant show, but courage was not enough. When Pickett led his men forward in their doomed charge, Meade's troops were primed and ready.

Early Life

George Gordon Meade was born in Spain on December 31, 1815. He was the ninth child of Richard and Christine Meade. Richard, the United States naval agent at Cadiz, heard the news in a Spanish jail cell. His crime? He had tried to collect on loans he had made to the king. Christine took her children back to Philadelphia when George was eighteen months old.

George attended a local school, then transferred to a military school. Richard, long since released from jail, died when George was twelve. His death left the family strapped for cash. Bright and good-humored, George went on to study at less-costly schools.

In 1831, Christine talked the secretary of war into giving the teenager an appointment to the United States Military Academy. Meade earned high marks, but disliked West Point's spit-and-polish discipline. When he graduated in 1835, he ranked nineteenth in a class of fifty-six. The new second lieutenant was a slender six-footer. He had brown hair, steely blue eyes, and a beaked nose.

Bored by army routines, Meade resigned in 1836. For the next five years, he worked as an engineer with the mapmaking U.S. Topographical Bureau. It was during this period that he met and married Margaret Sergeant. When he was away, which was often, Meade wrote to her every day.

In 1842, Meade lost his job because the bureau no longer employed civilians. His family helped him regain his army commission. During the Mexican War, he served with General Zachary Taylor's army in northern Mexico. After the war, Captain Meade helped build lighthouses on the Florida reefs. The army then put him in charge of making a geodetic survey of the Great Lakes. He was still engaged in that huge project when the Civil War began.

The Civil War

Many of Meade's fellow officers left the army to join the Confederacy. Meade was not one of them. He was pro-Union, even though he had close relatives in the South. On August 31, 1861, he pinned on the star of a brigadier general of Pennsylvania volunteers. The new general had never led troops in combat.

Meade spent the winter strengthening the Union lines around Washington. After that, he led a brigade during the Peninsula Campaign's invasion of Virginia in 1862. Perhaps he was new to combat, but he shared the front-line dangers with his men. The brigade fought in the Seven Days battles of Mechanicsville, Gaines's Mill, and Glendale. At Glendale, Meade was wounded twice. One bullet plowed through his forearm. A second lodged in his back near the hip. The wounds sent him home to Philadelphia, where Margaret nursed him back to health.

In September, Meade returned to action at Antietam, in Maryland. This was his first battle as division commander, and it was the bloodiest single day of the war. Three months later, he fought in the terrible defeat at Fredericksburg, Virginia. His division was the only Union force to penetrate the Southern lines that day. A promotion to major general gave Meade command of the Fifth Corps. At Chancellorsville in Virginia, he fought under General Joe Hooker in another losing battle. Back in Washington, President Lincoln knew it was time for Hooker to go.

At 3:00 A.M. on June 28, 1861, a colonel shook Meade awake. To lighten the moment, the man joked that he was bringing "trouble." Meade, half awake, assumed that Hooker had ordered his arrest. Instead, he was told that Lincoln had picked him to replace Hooker.[2]

The new commanding general was not well liked. Meade dressed sloppily, and his temper often flared out of control. Behind his back, his soldiers called him "the Snapping Turtle." During a battle, staff officers were reluctant to approach him, even when they carried vital reports. To his credit, Meade was brave, competent, and a quick learner. He moved swiftly and was not afraid to make tough decisions.

The new commander had no time to spare. Lee's army was sweeping through the Pennsylvania countryside. Meade pulled his forces together and took up the challenge. To safeguard Washington, he kept his army between Lee's troops and the Union capital. For a time, he planned to fight a defensive battle near Pipe Creek. The small crossroads town of Gettysburg lay just twenty miles away.

The largest battle ever fought in North America started on July 1, 1863. Union troops led by General John F. Reynolds tangled with a Southern force west of Gettysburg. By that afternoon, Union forces were digging in on Cemetery Ridge, east of Gettysburg. Three Union corps manned the defenses. In a midnight meeting, Meade agreed that this was the place to make a stand.

At dawn on July 2, Meade took control of his army. As the day wore on, he was dismayed to see General Daniel Sickle's corps leave a gap at the southern end of the Union lines. Meade was moving units to fill the gap when the Southerners attacked. General James Longstreet's men drove forward again and again, but the Union lines held firm. At Culp's Hill, the Union right wing beat back another Southern attack. That night, Meade made his prediction of a third assault on the center of his line.

On July 3, hard-fighting Northerners withstood the charge of General George Pickett's Virginians. Both attackers and defenders died by the thousands. Lee had attacked both flanks and the Union center—and Meade had countered every blow. The Southerners held their positions for a day to give their wagon trains a head start. Then they trudged south in a pouring rain.

Lincoln urged Meade to follow up his victory. He pointed out that the Potomac was in flood. With luck, Union forces might pin Lee and his army against the river. Meade counted his twenty-three thousand casualties and said his men were in no shape to mount a pursuit. Lincoln joined the chorus of critics who disagreed. They accused Meade of missing a priceless chance to end the war.[3]

The last half of 1863 dragged past. In the east, neither side made any decisive moves. In early 1864, U. S. Grant took over as the new general-in-chief. Instead of staying behind a desk, Grant chose to ride with his army. Meade still led the Army of the Potomac but ranked second to Grant.

When the army marched into Virginia, Grant made the major decisions. From the Wilderness campaign to Appomattox, Meade followed orders. Ever the good soldier, he made the best of the awkward arrangement. Grant, in turn, praised Meade for being a good team player.

Meade's Legacy

On May 23, 1865, Meade led his Army of the Potomac through Washington in a Grand Review. Children lined the streets and sang patriotic songs. For the first time in four years, the nation was at peace.

In 1864, General George Meade's Army of the Potomac invaded Virginia and fought a series of battles in the tangle of underbrush known as the Wilderness. In this old engraving, a heroic flagbearer has led Union troops directly into the Confederate lines. With no time to reload, soldiers on both sides fight with bayonets, clubbed rifles, and bare fists.

Meade remained in the army, a career soldier to the end. Assigned to command the Military District of the Atlantic, he made his headquarters in Philadelphia. The city purchased a home there for the war hero.

In 1868 and early 1869, Meade took on the thankless task of commanding the Department of the South. Washington expected him to enforce the harsh laws that governed life in the former Confederate states. Meade, however, had never hated Southerners. Now he did his best to soften the Reconstruction measures.

Harvard awarded the war hero an honorary doctorate of laws. One honor that escaped him was the rank of full general. In 1869, President Grant awarded the rank to Philip Sheridan, not to Meade. He also had to accept the judgment that he was a good general, not a great one. Bound by a defensive mind-set, he could not polish off a wounded opponent.[4]

In time, Meade's war wounds caused his health to fail. He died of pneumonia on November 6, 1872. After his death, Philadelphia collected $100,000 as a gift to his heirs. The city further honored him with a statue in Fairmount Park. That would have pleased the tough old soldier.

Philip Henry Sheridan
(1831–1888)

In his memoirs, General Philip Sheridan wrote that he was born March 6, 1831, at Albany, New York. His biographers disagreed. C. W. Donelson listed his birthplace as Boston, Massachusetts. Other writers said he was born in Somerset, Ohio. Until 1868 the *Army Register* listed Massachusetts as his birthplace, then switched it to Ohio.

Does it really matter where Sheridan was born? In the years after the Civil War, the answer was yes. War heroes were popular with voters, and many Republicans thought of the general as a leading candidate for president. To qualify, the Constitution said, he had to be a natural-born citizen.

John and Mary Sheridan were Irish immigrants. A child of theirs born outside the United States could

General Philip Henry Sheridan

not grow up to be president. After Sheridan's death, his family admitted that he had been born at sea. That simply opened a new chapter in the debate. If the ship had flown the British flag, Sheridan was born a British subject. If it had sailed under the Stars and Stripes, he was an American—and eligible for the White House.

The Republicans did not nominate Sheridan, so the case was never put to the test. What does matter is that the Sheridan boy grew up to become one of the great Civil War generals.

Early Life

After a brief stay in Albany, Philip Henry Sheridan's family moved to the frontier town of Somerset, Ohio. Road-building work often took John away from home for months at a time. The burden of raising the family fell on Mary.

Young Phil was far from handsome. The boy's large, bullet-shaped head rested on a short neck. His slender body and legs were short, his arms long. Dark blue eyes slanted down above a large nose. Neighborhood kids often taunted him. Phil's response was to fight—and whip—each bully in turn.

Phil started school at age ten but found classwork boring. On his own, he read and reread books on military history. Like many boys, he worked at odd jobs. At fourteen, he found a full-time job in a general store that paid twenty-four dollars a year. Honest and industrious, he worked his way up to head clerk.

In 1848, a friendly congressman gave Phil an appointment to the United States Military Academy. At eighteen, the new cadet stood only five feet five inches and weighed just 115 pounds. He made up for his poor math skills by studying late into the night. In his third year, Phil's hot temper almost cost him his career. Always alert to insults, he attacked a sarcastic cadet sergeant. West Point could have expelled him, but settled on a one-year suspension. Phil returned with his temper under control and graduated with the class of 1853.

The army sent Second Lieutenant Sheridan to Texas and then to the West Coast. In Oregon, he displayed courage under fire in a clash with American Indian raiders. That was not enough to win advancement in the peacetime army. After eight years, Sheridan was still a lowly lieutenant.

The Civil War

Once the Civil War started, Sheridan shot up in rank. Vacancies left by officers "going south" advanced him to captain in 1861. He served as a quartermaster under General Henry Halleck during the advance on Shiloh in Tennessee in 1862. That same spring, promoted to colonel, he took command of a Michigan cavalry unit.

Sheridan was fearless. He led by example, riding his big black horse directly into Confederate fire. In July, his regiment destroyed a supply train and tore up railroad tracks at Booneville, Mississippi. By

September, his exploits had earned him a promotion to brigadier general. The army added the second star of a major general in March 1863.

As 1863 dragged along, Sheridan's cavalry fought at Perryville and Murfreesboro, Tennessee. At Chickamauga in September, a doomed effort to anchor the Union right wing cost him fifteen hundred casualties. Two months later, his troopers redeemed themselves at Missionary Ridge near Chattanooga. With Sheridan's prodding, they clawed their way through heavy fire to the top of the ridge. The Confederates broke and ran, with the Northerners close at their heels.

The victory caught the eye of U. S. Grant. He took Sheridan with him when he headed east to command the Army of the Potomac in the spring of 1864. Grant needed a cavalry leader as tough as he was.

The army launched a massive drive on the Confederate capital at Richmond, Virginia, in May 1864. Sheridan was matched against General James Ewell Brown "Jeb" Stuart, the dashing Southern cavalry hero. A report reached Grant that Sheridan had boasted he could "thrash hell out of Stuart any day." Grant responded, "Well, he generally knows what he's talking about. Let him start out and do it."[1]

Sheridan set out with a column of ten thousand troops and horse-drawn artillery. He headed straight toward Richmond, hoping Stuart would attack. The plan worked. The Confederate cavalry, with only forty-five hundred men, charged Sheridan's forces at Yellow

Tavern. In the swirling battle, a Union private killed Stuart with a well-aimed pistol shot. The loss of Stuart hurt the South far more than the loss of the battle.

In July 1864, General Jubal Early's Confederate cavalry swept northeast through the Shenandoah Valley. The threat to the nation's capital was very real. Grant gave Sheridan forty-three thousand men and told him to close "the back door to Washington." Sheridan knew that stopping Early was only part of his job. He told his men to destroy the fields and herds that fed the Confederate army.

In September, Sheridan's Army of the Shenandoah trounced Early at Winchester and Fisher's Hill. True to their orders, his men also burned crops, houses, and barns. A crow flying across the valley, they laughed, would have to carry its own rations.

In early October, Sheridan was called to Washington for a meeting. While he was away, Early gathered his scattered forces. On October 19, he broke the Union lines with a stunning surprise attack. The Bluecoats fled from the field in panic. Sheridan had returned to Winchester the night before. Now, twenty miles from the battle, he heard the rumble of big guns. He leaped into his saddle and galloped toward the front. Before long, he found the road blocked by retreating troops. They forgot their panic when they saw him waving his hat. "Face the other way, boys!" Sheridan cried. "We are going back!"[2]

Inspired by his words, the men fell in behind him. By midafternoon, Sheridan had pulled his army

Sheridan's troopers left a trail of destruction behind when they swept through the Shenandoah Valley in the summer of 1864. Southern families packed up their belongings and fled for their lives. One woman wrote to her soldier husband, "If you put off coming [home] t'wont be no used to come, for we'll all . . . be out there in the garden in the graveyard with your ma and mine."

together. The Southerners had stopped to regroup, and his counterattack sent them reeling. Grant wired Lincoln, "Turning what bid fair to be a disaster into glorious victory stamps Sheridan, what I always thought him—one of the ablest generals."[3]

In March 1865, Sheridan sent George Armstrong Custer on a raid into northern Virginia. Custer won a brilliant victory, capturing sixteen hundred Confederates at a cost of only nine Union soldiers. Sheridan rode into Charlottesville a day later to accept the keys to the city from frightened citizens.

With the valley secure, Sheridan hurried back to the Union lines outside Petersburg. He found Grant discouraged by the long siege and the constant rain. Sheridan soon brightened the general-in-chief's mood. He urged Grant to let him attack Lee's weakened lines. "I tell you, I'm ready to strike out tomorrow and go to smashing things," he promised.[4]

Grant gave the cavalryman the orders he wanted. Once again, Sheridan was as good as his word. On April 1, his troops outflanked the Southern lines at Five Forks. The breakthrough opened the road to Richmond and Lee's surrender eight days later.

Sheridan's Legacy

After the war, Sheridan took command of the Military District of the Gulf. While the United States was engaged in its Civil War, France had installed a puppet king on the throne of Mexico.

Sheridan's show of force along the border helped speed the French withdrawal.

In March 1867, Sheridan served as military governor of Louisiana and Texas. True to his nature, he applied the harsh Reconstruction laws with a heavy hand. Grant stood behind him, but President Andrew Johnson did not. He removed Sheridan from his post.

In 1869, President Grant promoted his former comrade-in-arms to lieutenant general. Sheridan traveled to Europe, where he observed German troops in action during the Franco-Prussian War. In 1875, the forty-four-year-old Sheridan married twenty-two-year-old Irene Rucker. Irene later gave birth to three daughters and a son.

During the 1870s, Sheridan led the fight against the Plains Indians. His orders were to "make every Kiowa and Comanche knuckle down," and he followed these orders almost to the letter. At one point he sold the tribes' horses at auction and bought sheep with the money. The buffalo were vanishing, he said. It was time for nomadic hunters to settle down.[5]

Republicans talked of running Sheridan for president, but little came of it. He did receive one vote at the 1880 convention. In 1883, he took over as the army's general-in-chief. Five years later Congress promoted him to the rank of four-star general. The gesture almost came too late. Sheridan's weight had soared to more than two hundred pounds, and his heart was failing. He died at his Massachusetts seaside cabin a few months later, on August 5, 1888.

General William Tecumseh Sherman

William Tecumseh Sherman
(1820–1891)

On November 15, 1864, General William Tecumseh Sherman watched as Atlanta, Georgia went up in flames. The fires were no accident. Sherman had ordered his men to burn the city's factories and warehouses.

With the city burning behind them, Sherman's troops took a southeast route toward the ocean. Each of the army's four columns had orders to live "on the country." That meant stripping the land of food, horses, and forage. If they met resistance, officers were told to use deadly force.[1]

The Union columns cut a swath sixty miles wide through the heart of the state. When bands of Southern guerrillas harried them, the troops brushed them aside. The army's orders forbade needless destruction, but many Northern soldiers engaged in an orgy of burning and looting. "Sherman's bummers" swooped down on plantations and carried off food, livestock, bedding, and valuables.

On December 22, the army occupied Savannah. Behind it four hundred miles of hostile territory lay in ruins. Sherman sent a telegram to President Lincoln: "I beg to present you as a Christmas gift, the city of Savannah."[2]

Sherman's "March to the Sea" was far more than a tactical move. The fact that Union troops could trample their heartland dealt a crushing blow to Southern morale.

Early Life

On February 8, 1820, in Lancaster, Ohio, Charles and Mary Sherman welcomed the birth of a baby boy. Charles named him Tecumseh, after the famous Shawnee warrior. Years later, a priest added the name William when he baptized the boy. His ten brothers and sisters called him "Cump."

Charles Sherman died in 1829. Thomas Ewing, a well-to-do family friend, offered to raise one of the boys. He took nine-year-old Cump home to the Ewing mansion, less than one hundred yards away. Ewing, who went on to become a U.S. senator, sent the boy to Lancaster Academy. There the quick-witted redhead learned Latin, French, Greek, and arithmetic. At home, he struck up a close friendship with his foster sister, Ellen.

In 1836, Ewing offered Cump an appointment to the United States Military Academy. The sixteen-year-old jumped at the chance. He had grown up to be a tall, slim young man, with sunburned skin and piercing blue-gray eyes. As a cadet Cump excelled in the classroom but seldom kept his uniform clean. Despite a heavy load of demerits, he graduated sixth in the class of 1840.

Service in the South left the new second lieutenant with a deep love of the region. When the Mexican War broke out, he was posted to California. In 1848, his report to President Polk alerted the nation to the discovery of gold at Sutter's Mill. Back in Washington, his long courtship of Ellen Ewing ended in marriage. President Zachary Taylor was one of the wedding guests.

Sherman left the army in 1853 to enter business. For the rest of the decade he worked as a banker, as a lawyer, and as an educator. When Louisiana left the Union in April 1861, Sherman resigned as superintendent of the state military college (now Louisiana State University). He loved the South, but he loved the Union more.

The Civil War

In June 1861, Sherman rejoined the army with the rank of colonel. He was given little time to drill his recruits before they were thrown into the First Battle of Bull Run. One by one, his regiments broke under fire and fell back. A few days later, Lincoln came to speak to the disheartened troops. Sherman asked him not to lead any cheers. "We need cool, thoughtful, hard-fighting soldiers—no more hurrahing, no more humbug," he warned.[3]

That summer, Sherman earned the star of a brigadier general. The army sent him to Kentucky, where he took command of the Department of the Cumberland. Sherman almost caved in under the stress of his first major command. Convinced that his troops were outnumbered, he asked Lincoln for the impossible—two hundred thousand more men. He also feuded with reporters, who hit back by writing stories that hinted he was insane. After Sherman came close to suicide, the army sent him home to pull himself together.

Sherman returned to duty in February 1862. General U. S. Grant asked him to lead the Army of Tennessee's Fifth Division. That April, Sherman proved that he had regained his self-control. At the Battle of Shiloh he kept his raw troops in good order through two days of savage fighting. Sherman paid a price for his stay in the front lines. He had three horses shot from under him and ended the day with a hand wound. Afterward, Grant gave Sherman credit for the hard-won victory. With the praise came a promotion to major general.

The Union's heavy losses at Shiloh worried the folks at home. Critics assailed Grant for mismanaging his troops on the first day of the battle. When Grant talked of resigning, Sherman urged him to stay. The army needed leaders who were not easily rattled.

Grant turned to his friend when he wanted a tough job done. In December Sherman led thirty-two thousand troops against the Southern forces at Vicksburg, in Mississippi. Union gunboats covered his advance as he prepared to attack the defenders at Chickasaw Bluffs. Below the bluffs, the rugged terrain made his artillery useless. Sherman rashly ordered a frontal assault, only to see his men cut down by hidden gunners. Rather than risk further losses, he called off the attack.

Grant renewed the campaign against Vicksburg in May 1863. Sherman cut his Fifteenth Corps loose from its supply lines and headed east to Jackson. After defeating the small Southern force there, he turned back toward Vicksburg. From May 19 to 22, his troops battered the key river port's stubborn defenses. The corps then joined in the siege that forced the city to surrender on July 4.

At Chattanooga in late November, the Fifteenth Corps faced one of the South's best divisions. Soldiers fought bayonet to bayonet that day, and Sherman's men took a sound licking. He then made a forced march north to relieve a Union force that was trapped in Knoxville, Tennessee. News of his approach convinced the Southern general that it was time to lift the siege.

In March 1864, Grant was called east, and Sherman replaced him as commander of the Military

Department of the Mississippi. "Uncle Billy," as his men called him, now commanded all military operations in the west. He did not look the part. His uniform was almost always wrinkled and muddy. Cigar ash soiled his jacket, and his red hair was often uncombed. When it came to mastering the art of war, however, he had few equals.

Sherman moved south from Chattanooga in early May with one hundred thousand veteran troops. General Joe Johnston's Southerners, outnumbered two to one, fought a delaying action. Johnston fell back, dug in for a fight, then fell back again. His attempts to wear down Sherman simply prolonged the campaign.

By late July, Union troops were laying siege to Atlanta. Jefferson Davis, the Confederate president, had grown tired of Johnston's tactics. Davis ordered General John Hood to take command. Sherman quickly broke the back of Hood's counterattacks. On September 1, Hood abandoned Atlanta. Ten weeks later Sherman began his "March to the Sea."

On February 1, 1865, a well-rested Union army marched north from Savannah. As the troops advanced into South Carolina, they burned and looted with renewed fury. By mid-February Sherman's troops had taken Columbia, South Carolina. When General Johnston's weary troops tried to stand and fight, Sherman steamrollered over them.

Rather than let valuable properties fall into Northern hands, Southern troops destroyed many warehouses and factories before they withdrew from Atlanta in September 1864. Union troops finished the job before they followed General William Sherman eastward six weeks later. This photo shows that "Sherman's Bummers" already have demolished the railroad yard's stone roundhouse.

On April 18, Johnston surrendered at Durham Station, North Carolina. Four days earlier, Lincoln had been killed by John Wilkes Booth. As a result, enraged Northerners objected when Sherman paroled Johnston's soldiers and let them keep their horses, mules, and ten days' rations for the journey home. Sherman, it turned out, believed in a pitiless war and a merciful peace.

By May 24, tempers had cooled. Cheering crowds welcomed home Sherman and his troops as they marched through the capital in a Grand Review.

Sherman's Legacy

After the war, Sherman took command of the west with the rank of lieutenant general. When Grant became president in 1869, he gave Sherman the fourth star of a full general. As general-in-chief, Sherman wrote the orders that slowly and brutally forced the western American Indian tribes onto reservations. Sherman held the command for fourteen years until November 1883. He retired a year later.

Along with the "March to the Sea," Sherman is best remembered for two brief statements. During a speaking tour in 1880, he said, "Many look upon war as all glory, but it is all hell." Today, that line is often shortened to read "War is hell."

In 1884, voters were turning their backs on the Republicans. Party leaders talked about choosing Sherman to run for president. The crusty old general fired off a telegram to the convention: "I will not accept if nominated and will not serve if elected."[4]

In 1886, Sherman moved to New York City, where he enjoyed an active social life. He died there of pneumonia on February 24, 1891. Thirty thousand veterans escorted his coffin to the train station for the trip west to St. Louis.

General George Henry Thomas

George Henry Thomas
(1816–1870)

In December 1864, General John Hood led a Confederate army into Tennessee. His barefoot troops carried with them the South's last hopes. After they took a severe beating at Franklin, Hood ordered his troops to head for Nashville. Waiting behind the city's sturdy defenses was General George Thomas.

Thomas watched as Hood set up a siege line outside the city. The delay angered his superiors. U. S. Grant bombarded Thomas with telegrams that urged him to attack. Thomas, whose army was growing stronger by the day, refused to hurry. He liked to tell impatient officers, "The fate of a battle may depend on a buckle."[1]

On December 15, Thomas felt he was ready. His troops struck the Southerners with the force of a thunderbolt. Hood pulled his broken units back to a new line and tried to make a stand. Thomas hit him again the next day. Outnumbered and outgunned, the Southerners lost their nerve. The beaten troops did not end their retreat until they were safe in Mississippi.

Nashville was only the second time that a Southern army had broken and run. The first time was at Missionary Ridge outside Chattanooga. In each battle, the victors were led by George Thomas.

Early Life

George Henry Thomas was born in Southampton County, Virginia, on July 31, 1816. His parents, John and Mary Thomas, farmed the family homestead with the help of slaves. John died in a farm accident when George was fourteen. The broad-shouldered teenager took his place as the man of the family. During Nat Turner's slave revolt in 1831, his family fled into the woods. George rode from farm to farm, warning neighbors of the danger.

Mary encouraged her son to aim high. In 1834, an uncle made a place for him in his law office. George showed little interest in law, but in 1836 he found his life's work. A local congressman helped him gain entrance to the United States Military Academy.

Thomas impressed the staff at West Point by showing up weeks before the term began. This drive to prepare calmly and thoroughly for any task was a lifelong trait. Hazing was common at West Point, but no one picked on him more than once. The twenty-year-old six-footer weighed a muscular two hundred pounds. Long hours of study paid off at graduation. Thomas ranked twelfth in the class of 1840.

The army sent the new second lieutenant to an artillery unit. The posting opened the door to a long love affair with the big guns. Thomas saw his first combat in the war against the Seminoles. In the Mexican War, he won two battlefield promotions for gallantry.

Major Thomas returned to West Point in 1853 as an artillery instructor. There, at age thirty-six, he married Frances Kellogg. Two years later he joined the Second Cavalry and served on the Texas frontier. In 1860, a Comanche arrow lodged in his chest. He yanked the arrow out himself, then let a doctor dress the wound. During his six-month convalescence, Southern states began to leave the Union.

The Civil War

In March 1861, the governor of Virginia offered Thomas a key position in the state's volunteer forces. Thomas was torn between feelings of loyalty to his state and his sworn loyalty to his country. In the end he renewed his oath of allegiance to the United States. The decision outraged his sisters, who wrote to tell him he was no longer their brother.

The U.S. Army promoted Thomas to colonel. He fought briefly that summer in Virginia's Shenandoah

Valley. In August he was given the rank of brigadier general of volunteers and sent to Kentucky. In January 1862, at Mill Springs, his troops fought off a surprise attack and routed a strong Southern force. The victory opened the way for Union forces to pour into eastern Tennessee.

At Mill Springs and later, Thomas stood out on the battlefield. He liked to ride his big stallion along the front lines, sharing the danger with his soldiers. The men called him "Old Pap," a tribute to his cool, steady style. They knew he would do his best to keep them well fed and supplied. They also knew better than to abuse the stray dogs that gathered near his tent. Nothing angered Thomas more than seeing animals mistreated.

Thomas won lasting fame in September 1863 at Chickamauga Creek in Georgia. The battle began with Confederate general Braxton Bragg's sending men posing as deserters into the Union lines. The "deserters" fooled General William Rosecrans into thinking that Bragg was in full retreat. Rosecrans spread his three corps across a twenty-mile front and sent them in pursuit. Bragg sat back, hoping to smash the Union army one corps at a time.

"Old Pap" moved forward at his usual cautious pace. When scouts reported Bragg's real intentions, he shifted gears. Quickly, he pulled back his advance troops and dug in to receive an attack. Warning messages went out to the other corps. If Bragg had sprung his trap in time, the war in the west might have turned around. As it was, he held back and waited for reinforcements. Rosecrans gathered his army near Chickamauga Creek just in time.

When Bragg attacked on September 19, a mixup in orders opened a gap in the Union line. General James Longstreet's troops hit the gap and poured through. On one side, the Southerners pushed back a Union corps toward Chattanooga. On the other side, Thomas stood fast. His lines on Snodgrass Hill bent into a U-shape, but did not break. "Old Pap" seemed to be everywhere at once, moving troops to plug the weak spots. When powder and shot ran low, he growled, "Use your bayonets."[2]

The battle raged for five hellish hours. Behind the lines, General Gordon Granger grew tired of waiting for orders from Rosecrans. Acting on his own, he threw his reserve corps into the struggle. Thomas used the fresh troops to mount an attack that reclaimed some lost ground. Longstreet ordered assault after assault, but the Union lines did not break. Late in the day, a courier reached Thomas with orders to abandon the hill. He waited until dark, then organized a classic fighting retreat. Longstreet wrote later, "The Union army . . . melted away in our presence."[3]

Winners and losers each paid a high price. The Confederates lost 18,545 men killed, wounded, or missing. The North's losses numbered 16,179. What mattered most to the Union was that Thomas had saved Rosecrans and his army. Newspapers headlined

Union Soldiers, like their Southern counterparts, fought best when they admired and trusted their commanders. General George Thomas was one of those officers for whom men like the rifleman shown here would fight—and sometimes die. It was this kind of inspiring leadership that enabled Thomas to save a Union army in the Battle of Chickamauga.

the story and tagged Thomas as "the Rock of Chickamauga."

"Old Pap" had a second bright moment a month later in the battles that broke the siege of Chattanooga. On November 25, his troops opened the assault on the Southern strongpoint of Missionary Ridge by storming the defenses at the foot of the ridge. Then, scenting victory, they shouted, "Chickamauga!" and scrambled upward to drive the Southerners from the crest of the ridge. U.S. Grant, who had replaced Rosecrans, demanded to know who had ordered the charge. "When those fellows get started all hell can't stop them," an officer told him.[4]

In the aftermath of the battle, Thomas paused to bury the dead. He picked a hillside site and ordered his men to beautify it. When it came time for the burials, a chaplain asked Thomas if the graves should be organized by states. "No, no," he said. "Mix them up; mix them up. I am tired of state-rights."[5]

In May 1864, General William Sherman kicked off his Atlanta campaign. He relied on Thomas's Army of the Cumberland for half the invading force. Six months later Sherman launched his "March to the Sea." Thomas turned back with thirty-five thousand troops to defend Nashville. If he had failed, Hood's army would have had an open path northward.

After Thomas routed Hood's army, a grateful Congress promoted him to major general. Thomas believed the honor had been delayed because he was a Virginian. He told a friend, "It is better late than never, but it is too late to be appreciated. I earned this at Chickamauga."[6]

Thomas' Legacy

Thomas reviewed his troops one last time on May 9, 1865. Then he took command of the Department of the Cumberland. "Old Pap" won Nashville's hearts by putting his men to work as carpenters and painters. The war-torn city soon looked like new again. On a larger scale, Thomas did his best to rebuild the state governments of Tennessee, Kentucky, Mississippi, Alabama, and Georgia.

"Old Pap" never lowered his standards. When grateful citizens offered him gifts, he told them to give the money to the families of dead soldiers. He did unbend enough to pose for a $1,000 portrait by George Dury. He also accepted a gold medal struck in honor of the Battle of Nashville.

In June 1869 Thomas traveled to San Francisco to take command of the Pacific District. He was only fifty-three when he died there of a stroke on March 28, 1870. A fellow officer wrote, "He was a patriot without flaw and a soldier without reproach."[7] A modern writer went a step farther. He named Thomas, Grant, and Sherman as the three generals who won the war for the Union.

Military Units

During the Civil War, the North and the South organized their fighting forces according to a model in which progressively larger units were assigned increasing responsibilities. An order that originated at headquarters in Washington, D.C., or in Richmond, Virginia, would flow (→) step-by-step through this chain of command:

UNIT	DESCRIPTION
Army ↓	A combat and administrative unit assigned to a particular department of war. An army generally consists of a headquarters, two or more fighting corps, and the necessary support forces. *Commander*: a four-star general or a lieutenant general.
Corps ↓	A combat unit composed of two or more infantry divisions, plus artillery, cavalry, and support troops. *Commander*: a lieutenant general.
Division ↓	A combat unit (6,000 to 9,000 soldiers) made up of two or more brigades, self-contained and equipped for prolonged fighting. *Commander*: a major general.
Brigade ↓	A combat unit composed of a headquarters unit, two or more regiments of infantry, plus artillery, cavalry, and support units. *Commander*: a brigadier general or colonel.
Regiment ↓	A combat unit (1,000 or more soldiers) made up of at least two battalions. *Commander*: a colonel.
Battalion ↓	A combat unit consisting of a headquarters company and four or more infantry companies, artillery batteries, or similar units. *Commander*: a lieutenant colonel or a major.
Company ↓	A tactical or administrative unit (approximately thirty soldiers), made up of two or more platoons. *Commander*: a captain or a first lieutenant.
Platoon	The army's smallest tactical unit, composed of about twelve soldiers. *Commander*: a second lieutenant, assisted by a sergeant.

The Officer Corps

Armies depend on a corps of commissioned officers to guide and direct all phases of military operations. Success or failure often hinges on the skill, courage, and dedication of officers up and down the chain of command. Newly commissioned officers usually begin service as second lieutenants. Here's the path that leads upward from there, along with the insignia for each rank:

CATEGORY	RANK, INSIGNIA, and COMMAND RESPONSIBILITY
Line Officers *(Also called company grade officers or junior officers)*	Second lieutenants (gold bar)—assistant platoon commanders First lieutenants (silver bar)—platoon commanders and assistant company commanders Captains (two silver bars)—company commanders
Field Grade Officers *(Also called senior officers)*	Majors (gold oak leaf)—assistant battalion commanders Lieutenant colonels (silver oak leaf)—battalion commanders Colonels (silver eagle)—regiment and assistant brigade commanders
General Officers *(Confederate generals all wore three stars enclosed by an oak wreath.)*	Brigadier generals (one star)—brigade commanders Major generals (two stars)—division commanders Lieutenant generals (three stars)—corps and army commanders Generals (four stars)—army commanders

Note: In the hurly-burly of the Civil War, both sides assigned command responsibilities as dictated by circumstances. When officers of the proper rank were unavailable, lower-ranking officers often stepped in to take command of units their training and experience had not prepared them to lead. Both governments also made political appointments, some of which awarded high rank to men who were poorly qualified to lead soldiers into battle.

Glossary

abolitionist—Someone who worked to abolish slavery in the years before the Civil War.

ambush—A sudden or surprise attack made from a concealed position.

artillery—An army unit made up of cannons, their gunners, and transport for moving the guns.

assault—A large-scale attack launched against an enemy position.

barrage—A sustained period of artillery fire directed against enemy positions.

casualties—Military personnel killed, wounded, or missing in battle.

cavalry—In the 1800s, a highly mobile army unit trained to fight from horseback.

charge—A fast, determined assault against an enemy position.

Confederacy—The union of Southern states that fought for independence from the United States during the Civil War.

counterattack—A return assault made in response to an earlier enemy attack.

department—A geographic region, organized to support military operations.

deserters—Military personnel who leave their units without authorization.

dragoons—Heavily armed, mounted soldiers—i.e., cavalry troopers.

drill—The repetitious exercises used to train recruits to march in formation and use their weapons.

engineers—Military units trained to construct fortifications, bridges, railroads, and roads.

field hospital—A medical unit set up near a battlefield to care for casualties.

flank—The left or right side of a military unit's formation.

forts—Fortified defensive positions set up to defend important towns, cities, ports, and farmlands.

frontier—A thinly populated area on the edge of a settled region.

gallantry—Heroic behavior in battle. Armies recognize gallantry by awarding medals.

guerrillas—Fast-moving armed bands that operate outside the normal laws of warfare.

infantry—Combat units trained to fight on foot.

offensive—A military maneuver designed to advance into enemy territory.

outflank—A tactic that puts troops in position to attack an enemy's vulnerable flanks.

outpost—An outlying military post, usually held by a small number of troops.

parole—An agreement that releases a prisoner of war, based on the prisoner's promise not to fight again.

pontoon bridge—A temporary floating structure that allows troops to cross a river.

quartermaster—The officer in charge of supplying food, clothing, and equipment to a military unit.

rangers—During the Civil War, soldiers trained to patrol and defend an area, usually from horseback.

rear guard—Troops sent to slow or stop an enemy advance, thus giving their own army a chance to retreat.

recruits—Volunteers and draftees who must be trained before they can be sent into battle.

retreat—The process of pulling back from a fortified position.

secession—The act of withdrawing from a political alliance.

sentry—A soldier or sailor who stands guard at an assigned position.

shrapnel—Deadly chunks of metal hurled through the air by an exploding shell.

siege—A prolonged attack that traps defenders within a fortified position.

skirmish—A small-scale clash between forward units of opposing armies.

stockade—A defensive wall made of poles set upright in the ground.

strategy—A military plan calculated to win a battle, a campaign, or a war.

supply line—The route over which supplies move to an army at the front.

tactics—The maneuvers an army uses to carry out its strategy.

troopers—A term often applied to soldiers who ride with a cavalry unit.

truce—An agreement to suspend fighting while peace talks go on.

Union—The states that remained loyal to the federal government during the Civil War.

wagon train—Transport vehicles used by an army to carry ammunition, food, supplies, and casualties.

wings—The units assigned to the left and right sides of an army's position in the field.

Chapter Notes

Chapter 1

1. Robert Leckie, *None Died in Vain; The Saga of the American Civil War* (New York: HarperCollins, 1990), p. 207.

2. Ben P. Poore, *The Life and Public Services of Ambrose E. Burnside* (Providence: J. A. & R. A. Reid, 1882), p. 194.

3. Leckie, *None Died in Vain*, p. 413.

4. T. Harry Williams, *The Union Restored, Vol. 6 of The Life History of the United States* (New York: Time, 1963), p. 57.

Chapter 2

1. Roy Merdedith, *Mr. Lincoln's General, U. S. Grant* (New York: Dutton, 1959), p. 22.

2. Thomas Pitkin, ed., *Grant the Soldier* (Washington, D.C.: Acropolis Books, 1965), pp. 33–34.

3. Bruce Catton, *Grant Moves South* (Boston: Little, Brown, 1960), p. 371.

4. Pitkin, *Grant the Soldier*, p. 47.

5. Bruce Catton, *A Stillness at Appomattox* (Garden City, N.Y.: Doubleday, 1953), p. 39.

6. Ibid., p. 133

7. Pitkin, *Grant the Soldier*, p. 72.

Chapter 3

1. Ezra J. Warner, *Generals in Blue* (Baton Rouge: Louisiana State University Press, 1964), p. 196.

2. Mark M. Boatner III, *The Civil War Dictionary* (New York: David McKay Company, 1959), p. 367.

3. Robert Leckie, *None Died in Vain; the Saga of the American Civil War* (New York: HarperCollins, 1990), p. 214.

4. Warner, *Generals in Blue*, p. 196.

5. Ibid.

Chapter 4

1. David M. Jordan, *Winfield Scott Hancock: A Soldier's Life* (Bloomington: Indiana University Press, 1988), pp. 129–130.

2. Ronald H. Bailey, *Forward to Richmond: McClellan's Peninsular Campaign* (Alexandria, Va.: Time-Life Books, 1983), p. 113.

3. Glenn Tucker, *Hancock the Superb* (Indianapolis: Bobbs-Merrill, 1960), p. 133.

4. Ibid., p. 151.

Chapter 5

1. Robert Leckie, *None Died in Vain; The Saga of the American Civil War* (New York: HarperCollins, 1990), p. 424–425.

2. Ezra J. Warner, *Generals in Blue* (Baton Rouge: Louisiana State University Press, 1964), p. 233.

3. Walter H. Hebert, *Fighting Joe Hooker* (Indianapolis: Bobbs-Merrill, 1944), p. 49.

4. Ibid., pp. 144–145.

5. T. Harry Williams, *The Union Restored, Vol. 6 of The Life History of the United States* (New York: Time, Inc., 1963), p. 59.

6. Leckie, *None Died in Vain*, p. 472.

7. Ibid., p. 422.

Chapter 6

1. Gabor S. Borritt, *Lincoln's Generals* (New York: Oxford University Press, 1994), p. 10.

2. Robert Leckie, *None Died in Vain; The Saga of the American Civil War* (New York: HarperCollins, 1990), p. 188.

3. Geoffrey C. Ward, *The Civil War: An Illustrated History* (New York: Knopf, 1990), p. 152.

Chapter 7

1. George R. Stewart, *Pickett's Charge* (Greenwich, Conn.: Fawcett, 1963), p. 59.

2. Robert Leckie, *None Died in Vain; The Saga of the American Civil War* (New York: HarperCollins, 1990), p. 485.

3. David Herbert Donald, *Lincoln* (New York: Simon & Schuster, 1995), pp. 446–447.

4. T. Harry Williams, *The Union Restored, Vol. 6 of The Life History of the United States* (New York: Time, 1963), pp. 12–13.

Chapter 8

1. Roy Morris, Jr., *Sheridan: The Life and Wars of General Phil Sheridan* (New York: Crown Publishers, 1992), p. 164.

2. Lawrence A. Frost, *The Phil Sheridan Album* (Seattle: Superior, 1968), p. 80.

3. Ibid., p. 81.

4. Morris, *Sheridan,* p. 244.

5. Ibid., pp. 344–347.

Chapter 9

1. Joseph B. Mitchell, *Military Leaders in the Civil War* (New York: G. P. Putnam's Sons, 1972), p. 167.

2. Gabor Boritt, *Lincoln's Generals* (New York: Oxford University Press, 1994), p. 156.

3. B. A. Botkin, ed., *A Civil War Treasury of Tales, Legends, and Folklore* (New York: Random House, 1960), p. 12.

4. John F. Marszalek, *Sherman: A Soldier's Passion for Order* (New York: Maxwell Macmillan, 1995), p. 453.

Chapter 10

1. Col. Red Reeder, *The Northern Generals* (New York: Duell, Sloan and Pearce, 1964), p. 188.

2. Fairfax Downey, *Storming of the Gateway: Chattanooga, 1863* (New York: David McKay, 1960), p. 125.

3. Jerry Korn, *The Fight for Chattanooga: Chickamauga to Missionary Ridge* (Alexandria, VA: Time-Life Books, 1985), p. 72.

4. T. Harry Williams, *The Union Restored, Vol. 6 of The Life History of the United States* (New York: Time, 1963), p. 101.

5. B. A. Botkin, ed., *A Civil War Treasury of Tales, Legends, and Folklore* (New York: Random House, 1960), p. 334.

6. Henry Coppée, *General Thomas* (New York: D. Appleton, 1912), p. 286.

7. David Nevin, *Sherman's March* (Alexandria, Va.: Time-Life Books, 1986), pp. 124–125.

Index